D040652

She
Persisted

···

ROSALIND FRANKLIN

···

—INSPIRED BY—

She Persisted

by Chelsea Clinton & Alexandra Boiger

· ·

ROSALIND
FRANKLIN

· · · · · · · · · · · · · · · · · · · ——— · · · · · · · · · · · · · · · ·

Written by
Kimberly Brubaker Bradley

Interior illustrations by
Gillian Flint

PHILOMEL

ↂ *To* ↄ

Dorothy Hamilton, Sharon Palmer,
and Virginia White, the chemistry professors at
Smith College whom I studied under. Thank you!

PHILOMEL BOOKS
An imprint of Penguin Random House LLC, New York

First published in the United States of America by Philomel Books,
an imprint of Penguin Random House LLC, 2022

Text copyright © 2022 by Chelsea Clinton
Illustrations copyright © 2022 by Alexandra Boiger

Philomel Books is a registered trademark of Penguin Random House LLC.

Visit us online at penguinrandomhouse.com.

Library of Congress Cataloging-in-Publication Data is available.

Printed in the United States of America

HC ISBN 9780593402979
10 9 8 7 6 5 4 3 2 1
PB ISBN 9780593402993
10 9 8 7 6 5 4 3 2 1

WOR

Edited by Talia Benamy and Jill Santopolo.
Design by Ellice M. Lee.
Text set in LTC Kennerley.

The publisher does not have any control over and does not assume any responsibility
for author or third-party websites or their content.

Dear Reader,

As Sally Ride and Marian Wright Edelman both powerfully said, "You can't be what you can't see." When Sally said that, she meant that it was hard to dream of being an astronaut, like she was, or a doctor or an athlete or anything at all if you didn't see someone like you who already had lived that dream. She especially was talking about seeing women in jobs that historically were held by men.

I wrote the first *She Persisted* and the books that came after it because I wanted young girls—and children of all genders—to see women who worked hard to live their dreams. And I wanted all of us to see examples of persistence in the face of different challenges to help inspire us in our own lives.

I'm so thrilled now to partner with a sisterhood of writers to bring longer, more in-depth versions of these stories of women's persistence and achievement to readers. I hope you enjoy these chapter books as much as I do and find them inspiring and empowering.

And remember: If anyone ever tells you no, if anyone ever says your voice isn't important or your dreams are too big, remember these women. They persisted and so should you.

Warmly,

Chelsea Clinton

She
Persisted

ROSALIND FRANKLIN

TABLE OF CONTENTS

······························

A Curious Child

From the very start, Rosalind Franklin loved to figure things out. She loved word puzzles. She loved the memory games her father played with her and her older brother. She loved arithmetic, so much so that when she was six years old and her family went on a vacation to the seashore, she spent her free time on the beach with a paper and pencil, writing out math problems and solving them.

Rosalind was born on July 25, 1920, to a well-off family in London, England. She had an older brother; later, she would have two younger brothers and a younger sister. Rosalind's parents loved each other and their children very much, though they weren't the kind of family that hugged and kissed very often. Instead they took hikes together, played games, and worked together to support ideas that were important to them.

When he was growing up, Rosalind's father had wanted to study science at either Oxford or Cambridge, England's oldest and most well-known universities. But World War I started just before he would have enrolled. Instead of becoming a student, Ellis Franklin joined the army and fought for his country. By the time the war was over, he had a wife and a son, and he decided it was too late for him to go back to school. Instead he worked at the merchant bank his family ran. He still loved science, and he loved to help people. Several nights a week, he taught classes in electricity and magnetism at the Working Men's College in London, a school for older adults.

Rosalind and her family were Orthodox Jews. At that time most people in England were Christians. Many people were prejudiced against Jews. They treated them unfairly because they were different. Prejudice against Jewish people is called antisemitism. Among other things, antisemitism in England meant that Jewish people usually weren't appointed to high positions in government or education. Rosalind's family broke some of these antisemitic barriers. One of her great-grandfathers was the first Jewish professor at an English university. Her father's uncle was the first Jew to serve on Britain's Cabinet, and Rosalind's own uncle was attorney general of the British mandate of Palestine. When Adolf Hitler rose to power in Nazi Germany during the 1930s and began terrorizing German Jews, Rosalind's family helped many of them escape to England and start new lives there. Still, even though Rosalind's family held important positions and did good things, many people disliked them just because they were Jews.

When Rosalind grew older, she decided that while she believed in God as a creator, she didn't believe in the parts of religion that didn't sound logical or concrete to her. Rosalind liked logic and concrete answers. But being Jewish was always important to her. She loved the traditions she grew up with. She also always felt that being Jewish meant she had an obligation to live a good life and contribute to creating a better world.

Rosalind and her siblings had a nanny (they called her "Nannie") to help feed them and dress them and take them to the park every day. There were other people who worked for her family, who cooked meals, did laundry, and cleaned their home. Rosalind's grandparents had a large home in the countryside, with a croquet lawn and tennis courts, and Rosalind often spent time with her cousins there. The first years of Rosalind's life were surrounded by luxury, comfort, and love.

Then, when she was eight years old, Rosalind became seriously ill with an infection. This was before the discovery of antibiotics, and infections could be very difficult to treat. Rosalind was sick for a long time. Even when she recovered, she remained frail and weak. Rosalind's parents decided to send her away to boarding school on the coast of England. They hoped the sea air would be healthier for her than London's wintertime pollution and Rosalind could regain her strength.

The school was called Lindores School for

Young Ladies. Rosalind went there right after her sister, Jennifer, was born. She was terribly homesick. She missed the new baby and her three brothers—David, Colin, and Roland—and her parents and her home. She felt it was unfair that she was sent away. She became healthy, swimming and playing field hockey and other outdoor games, and she returned to London after two school terms, but she never forgot how isolated she felt at boarding school. For the rest of her life, Rosalind hated the very *idea* of being sick. She always, always told her family she felt fine.

Once she returned to London, Rosalind began attending St. Paul's Girls' School. St. Paul's was a very good school, one of the first in England to teach girls all the same subjects boys usually learned. In addition to Latin, German, and French,

St. Paul's taught physics, chemistry, and calculus. St. Paul's girls also played a lot of sports, which Rosalind loved. And St. Paul's was a day school, not a boarding school, which meant Rosalind was back living at home with her family.

Rosalind was very happy. The only thing she didn't like about St. Paul's was the music classes—she was so bad at singing that the music teacher asked her parents if perhaps she had a hearing problem! (She didn't.)

Rosalind studied hard and was usually the top student in her class. She was passionate, intense, and always curious. She loved to learn. She loved to discover things. By the time she was fifteen, Rosalind had made up her mind: she was going to become a scientist!

....

CHAPTER 2

Choosing Her Path

There had been accomplished and famous woman scientists in the past—Ada Lovelace, Maria Mitchell, and others—but they were rare. For a long time, scientific discoveries were mostly considered curiosities instead of ways to improve peoples' lives. Science was a hobby, something rich people did for fun, fitting it around families and travel and other, more serious interests. It was not a job.

That had completely changed by 1935, when Rosalind was fifteen. Scientific discoveries such as electric lights, combustion engines, refrigerators, and telephones had made enormous differences in the world. Science was now taken very seriously, and scientists were well-paid professionals. But the more mainstream scientific study became, the fewer women pursued it.

Science became a job more than a hobby, and at that time, well-off women—such as Rosalind was, because of the family she was born into—were not expected to hold jobs. Lower-income women sometimes had no choice but to work full time—after all, the people who worked in Rosalind's family home were mostly women. Wealthier women were encouraged to do volunteer work—to help their communities without being paid. Rosalind's mother, aunts, and grandmother all did. But the kind of scientific study that intrigued Rosalind most required an advanced education and expensive equipment. It couldn't really be done as a volunteer.

Many people thought women shouldn't work if they could afford not to. A woman working in an important profession was seen as taking that job away from the imaginary man who might have held it otherwise. Even when women did pursue careers, they were expected to choose ones that didn't require advanced study—to become nurses, not doctors; village schoolteachers, not college professors. The famous universities of Oxford and Cambridge had started to allow a few women to enroll as students, but at that time, Cambridge didn't give woman graduates real degrees. The women took the same classes as the men, did the same work, took the same tests, and earned the same grades—but they didn't end up with the same recognition or the same amount of power.

It was also still rare for women to attend university, and even more rare for them to study science. Across all of England at that time, not one single woman held a major university job in any of the sciences. The famed Royal Society of Science, which had funded research in England since the 1600s, had several hundred male members—and not one woman.

Still, Rosalind expected her family to be pleased by her ambition. After all, her own father was sorry that he hadn't been able to become a scientist. Surely he would understand.

Rosalind's father disappointed her. As she prepared for her challenging final years of study at

St. Paul's—ones only taken by girls who planned to go to university—he told her she should study how to help the poor instead. That way, instead of holding down a paid job, she'd be able to volunteer to help other women, like the Jewish refugees now arriving from Germany. After all, she didn't need to earn her own money. Rosalind's parents were happy to support her until she found a husband who could.

Rosalind was furious. Her family had always taken her seriously before. Now they seemed to think that she was too young to know what she wanted to do. Plus, she knew she would be *terrible* at a job that mostly involved people. Rosalind liked problems that had concrete answers. People could be confusing. They were much harder for her to understand.

Rosalind felt that her father only said this because she was a girl. It made her unhappy. He changed his mind and allowed her to study whatever she pleased—but she never forgot that he'd doubted her. Rosalind knew that if her father thought her becoming a scientist was a bad idea, other people would too.

She didn't let those doubts stop her. She persisted. Rosalind graduated as the top student in her class at St. Paul's. She won a scholarship—money to help pay for college. Her parents insisted she give it to a student who actually needed the money. They paid her tuition instead.

Rosalind Franklin enrolled at Cambridge University in the autumn of 1938. She was on her way to making her dream come true.

CHAPTER 3

Studying Science During a War

In fall of 1938, when Rosalind was about to start classes at Cambridge, German leader Adolf Hitler, who had already invaded Austria, threatened to invade Czechoslovakia. England didn't want him to do that, but the only way to stop him was to go to war against him, and England really didn't want another war. Over a million British soldiers had died in World War I less than twenty years before. No one in England wanted to fight again.

England's prime minister went to talk to Hitler. People all over England waited anxiously. Rosalind's classes at Cambridge were delayed until word came back: the leaders of England and Germany had signed a peace treaty.

Many people were happy, but others thought war had only been delayed, not prevented. Life at Cambridge quickly began to change. Students studying science and medicine weren't drafted into the armed services (women, though they weren't drafted to fight, were drafted to serve in other ways). But many of their professors left to do war work—secret work, mostly, about weapons and radar and defense. Rosalind and her fellow students had to be more independent than usual. For Rosalind that was no trouble at all. She often worked in her laboratory all day.

Rosalind didn't always get along with the teachers who were left. One of them thought she was *too* independent, and too stubborn as well. Rosalind thought that he just didn't like it when female students argued with him. Rosalind loved to argue. She loved to say what she thought and listen to what other people thought. It helped her make decisions. She didn't argue because she was angry—to her it was just a way to exchange information. Sometimes other people didn't see it like that.

Rosalind studied physical chemistry, the sort of chemistry that concentrates on the rules and shapes and behaviors of molecules. Molecules are tiny pieces of matter. They're made up of individual atoms. You can think of atoms as letters of the alphabet, and molecules as words. Both the letters that you choose and the way you put them together are important. The letters O, P, S, and T can combine to make STOP, POTS, TOPS, and OPTS. Some combinations, like OSPT, don't make words—the letters can't combine that way.

Some molecules, like water, are made of only a few atoms. Others, like proteins, can be made of hundreds or even thousands of atoms. All molecules are incredibly small. There are more than a billion water molecules in one single drop of water! Every time you drink a glass of water, you're drinking ten times as many molecules of water as there are stars in the universe. It's amazing!

Physical chemistry is chemistry plus physics plus math. It's difficult and complicated. Rosalind loved it.

At the start of Rosalind's second year of college, England joined the war against Germany. At home, Rosalind's parents took in a Jewish refugee her sister's age who lived with the Franklins for several years until she could be reunited with her family at the end of the war. As the war went on, food and fuel and even clothing became hard to find. Travel was restricted. At night, people covered their windows with dark cloth to hide from airplanes carrying bombs. Many cities, especially

London, were badly damaged by bombs anyway. Cambridge was one of the few cities that never was.

Rosalind worked hard. Her one disappointment came right at the end of her time at Cambridge. Rosalind very much wanted to earn the top degree, called a first-class degree. Rosalind worked and studied so hard that when it came time to take her exams, she was utterly exhausted. She didn't do as well as she might have. She was disappointed with her high-second-class honors. However, most people thought that was an achievement. Rosalind earned a scholarship to continue her studies as a graduate student. This time, she took it.

In 1942 Rosalind began graduate work at Cambridge, studying under a man named Ronald George Wreyford Norrish. He was a very good scientist. In 1967, he would win the Nobel Prize in

Chemistry, the top award a scientist could earn. But he was not a very nice person. Like Rosalind, he was stubborn and argumentative. But while he liked to argue with other people, he disliked it very much when other people argued back. He recognized that Rosalind was bright and ambitious. He didn't like that she expected to be treated on an equal basis with the male chemists in the laboratory.

To Rosalind, this was simply ridiculous. She thought she deserved to be judged only on the quality of her work, not on whether she was a man or a woman. She called Ronald Norrish an "ogre."

It was still wartime, and by now Rosalind needed to be working for the war effort anyhow. She moved to a laboratory near London, where she worked for the government studying the physical chemistry of coal. Ronald Norrish still officially supervised Rosalind, but now she didn't have to be around him every day. She worked on her own. During the day she did research. In the evenings she worked as an air raid warden, warning people of incoming bomb attacks and getting them help if they were bombed.

Coal might seem like a strange thing to study during a war, but it was important. Coal was the main fuel used in England, and the only fuel the country produced itself. Coal comes from plants that died a long time ago. Since it comes from lots of different kinds of plants, there are lots of different kinds of coal, but when you look at pieces of coal, they all look the same.

Rosalind studied the way atoms arranged themselves in different kinds of coal. She learned how tiny spaces between the atoms changed the way coal behaved. She learned how to tell different kinds of coal apart. That way, industries could use the type that best suited them. It was careful, important work. It earned Rosalind a doctorate degree from Cambridge in 1945.

Then the Allies defeated Hitler. The long,

hard war was over in Europe. Rosalind's studies were complete, and she was no longer tied to her war service research. She was Dr. Rosalind Franklin, PhD. She could work wherever she chose.

....

Learning About X-rays

Rosalind went to France. She spoke French well and had always loved the country, which she'd visited before the war. She once told a friend that she sometimes felt more French than English—at least, she often got along better with French people. Rosalind found that French scientists enjoyed arguing, just like she did, and they didn't have as many silly ideas about how women should behave.

Rosalind worked in a laboratory in Paris. Unlike London, Paris hadn't been badly damaged during the war. All its elegant buildings were still standing. But food and housing were scarce and expensive. Rosalind found a small room for rent on the fifth floor of a building. She rode her bicycle along the river to get to work each day.

She was learning a new way to study molecules called X-ray diffraction.

There are a lot of different kinds of energy. One type, electromagnetic energy, exists as waves.

Think of the waves you might see in a puddle of water on a windy day. The surface of the water moves up and down. The waves have a high point and a low point. If you measure the distance between the high point of one wave and the high point of the next wave, you get their wavelength.

If you measure how fast the waves move, you get their frequency. Waves with short wavelengths have high frequency. Waves with long wavelengths have low frequency, like this:

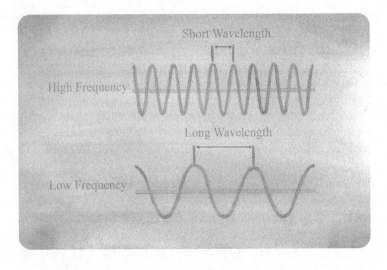

Just like water waves, electromagnetic waves have wavelength and frequency. There are many different kinds of electromagnetic waves. Radio waves can have wavelengths several feet long! They have very low frequency. Visible light has medium wavelengths and medium frequencies. X-rays have very small wavelengths and very high frequencies.

Diffraction is the way waves act when they hit something. They bounce back. They bounce off each other and change.

Scientists already knew that X-rays could be used to make photographs of people's bones. The X-rays' wavelength was so small that it could go through soft tissue, like skin and muscle. X-rays bounced off harder tissue, like bones. The bouncing wavelengths could be captured on a photograph. It was the first time doctors could see inside a human body without cutting into it.

Not long before Rosalind Franklin went to France, scientists realized that X-rays could be used another way. Their wavelengths could be made smaller than the distances between atoms in a molecule. If you fired X-rays at a molecule and looked at the pattern of the waves that bounced back, you could learn something about the structure of the molecule.

This was very important. Scientists already understood the structure of many simple molecules. After all, when a molecule was made of only a few atoms, there weren't very many choices. A water molecule, for example, was made of two hydrogen atoms and one oxygen. Hydrogen atoms can only attach to one other atom, so the structure of water had to be H-O-H.

Penicillin, the first antibiotic, is made up of sixteen carbon atoms, eighteen hydrogen atoms, four oxygen atoms, two nitrogen atoms, and one atom of sulfur. Imagine these atoms as a pile of forty-one LEGO bricks. There are hundreds of ways they could fit together! But until scientists knew the correct structure of penicillin, they wouldn't be able to manufacture it—and penicillin had become a very important medicine. X-ray diffraction revealed its structure. The structure of penicillin was discovered by another famous British woman scientist, Dorothy Crowfoot Hodgkin. She would win the Nobel Prize in Chemistry in 1964.

X-ray diffraction was new and difficult to do. Everything happened on such a tiny scale. Remember how small molecules are? Penicillin molecules were pretty big, and still one shot of penicillin contained 5,000,000,000,000,000,000,000 molecules. X-ray diffraction meant taking photographs of the waves bouncing in the spaces *between* the atoms of the molecules.

Rosalind wasn't studying penicillin. She was back to studying different kinds of coal. Now she was using X-ray diffraction. When she was successful, she ended up with a photograph that looked like this:

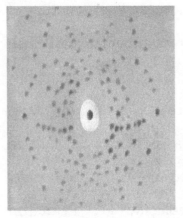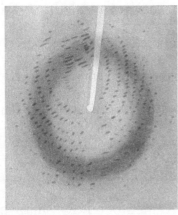

These photos gave important information to the people who understood them. Rosalind had to sit down with each photo, measure the distances and angles between all the dots, and do a lot of math. Eventually the math would lead her to the structure of the molecule. It was not easy, and it took a long time. Dorothy Crowfoot Hodgkin, who discovered penicillin's structure, worked thirty-five years to discover the structure of insulin, another important molecule.

Rosalind enjoyed X-ray crystallography, which was the name for this new branch of science. It was picky and precise. It suited her strengths. But the early diffraction machines leaked radiation. This could be dangerous. X-rays were small enough that they could enter cells in the human body and make tiny changes. Too much exposure to X-rays caused cancer.

Scientists knew this. They wore badges that measured how much radiation they were exposed to. If the badge showed they were over a safe limit, they had to quit working for a few weeks. Rosalind was unhappy when overexposure kept her away from the lab. She wasn't too worried about radiation. She wanted to work.

Rosalind thought about staying in France, but her family missed her and she missed them. In 1951, after four years, she left Paris and went back to England. She took a job in a research laboratory at King's University, in London. There she helped make a discovery that changed the world. She used X-ray diffraction to photograph DNA.

· ·

CHAPTER 5

A Crucial Discovery

You might not realize it, but you already know a lot about DNA. You know that traits like eye color or height can be inherited. You know that tomato seeds will always grow into tomato plants, which will in turn produce other tomatoes with their own seeds. Tomato seeds will never grow corn. In the same way, dogs will always have puppies, not kittens—and the puppies will resemble their parents. You know these things without thinking about them very hard—but they're true because of a substance called DNA.

DNA stands for deoxyribonucleic acid. (You can see why we just call it DNA!) Every cell—plant or animal or human—contains DNA, usually tightly coiled into chromosomes, which come in pairs. An offspring gets one of each pair of chromosomes from each parent. Humans usually have twenty-three pairs of chromosomes, for a total of forty-six. Mice have twenty pairs. Tomatoes have twelve.

DNA is the blueprint of every living thing. But in 1950, no one really understood what it *was*. Scientists knew it was an enormous molecule. They knew it consisted of three parts: phosphate groups, sugars, and nitrogen bases. There were four different types of nitrogen bases, called adenine, guanine, cytosine, and thymine. The amount of adenine in a segment of DNA always equaled the amount of thy-mine. The amount of cytosine always equaled the amount of guanine. But scientists didn't know how the three parts were put together. Understanding the structure of DNA would unlock an entire new branch of biology. It would change the world, and scientists knew it. All across the globe, researchers were studying DNA.

Rosalind Franklin came to King's College, London, in January 1951 to work in the X-ray diffraction laboratory run by a man named John Randall. Another man there named Maurice Wilkins was already working on DNA with old, outdated equipment. Randall let Rosalind install newer equipment. She spent the first eight months just setting it up.

Rosalind was friendly with everyone in the

lab except Maurice Wilkins. They disliked each other right way. Wilkins was quiet and shy. He didn't like loud people, and Rosalind was certainly loud. He'd also been struggling to discover a way to keep his DNA samples in a form that made them easier to photograph. Rosalind not only told him how to do it, she told him the technique had been discovered a long time ago. Maurice was embarrassed.

They quit disliking each other. They *despised* each other.

Meanwhile, back at Cambridge, two scientists named James Watson and Francis Crick were also working on the structure of DNA, and so was a famous scientist in America named Linus Pauling.

In November of 1951, eleven months after she returned to London, Rosalind gave a lecture

about her research. James Watson traveled from Cambridge to hear it. Rosalind showed early photographs of the X-ray diffraction of DNA and concluded that DNA formed helices—that is, it spiraled around itself—with the phosphate groups on the outside.

James didn't take notes or listen very carefully. Nor did he believe Rosalind's theory. A few months later, he and Francis proposed a DNA structure that had the phosphate groups on the inside. (Linus Pauling thought they were on the inside of the molecule, too.)

It was tricky and complicated work. The math needed to interpret the photographs was difficult and took a long time. Plus, it turned out that DNA could take two different shapes—Rosalind called them the A form and the B form. This meant that the results from one photograph didn't always match the results from another.

Rosalind persisted. In May 1952, she and her research assistant, Raymond Gosling, were able to take a beautifully clear X-ray photograph of the B form of DNA. It was the best of their many attempts. They labeled it Photo 51.

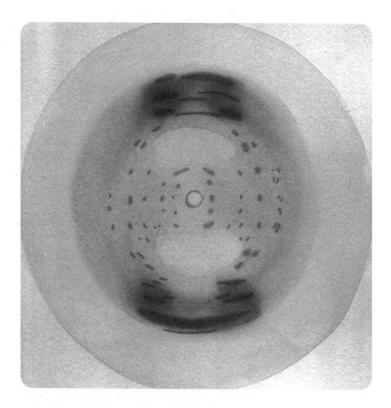

It doesn't look like much to us, but to Rosalind Franklin it proved DNA's structure: not simply a helix, but a *double* helix—two spirals joined in the middle by the nucleotide bases.

Rosalind continued working on mathematical proof. She also started looking for a different job. She didn't want to work with Maurice Wilkins anymore.

John Randall, Rosalind's boss, told the researchers at Cambridge about Rosalind's work. On January 30, 1953, James Watson came to Cambridge to talk about it. He and Rosalind ended up having an argument about DNA. James thought Rosalind's structure was wrong. Maurice Wilkins, though he still hated Rosalind, knew she was right. As James Watson was leaving, Maurice Wilkins secretly showed him Photo 51. When James saw it, he later wrote, "My mouth fell open and my pulse began to race." But to really understand the photo, James also needed Rosalind's calculations, which he was able to get and read.

Maurice never told Rosalind he shared her photograph. He didn't ask her permission to share it. A few weeks later, Rosalind took a new job at Birkbeck College. She had to leave all her DNA research photos, and many of her notes, at King's College—they belonged to the laboratory, not to her. But before she left, she wrote a scientific paper about her discovery and sent it to be published.

Scientists use scientific papers to share knowledge. They also do it to claim ownership of their discoveries. The first person to publish a discovery gets the credit for it.

James Watson and Francis Crick beat Rosalind

to it. As soon as they saw Rosalind's photograph, they changed their theory of DNA's structure. Like her, they now believed it to be a double helix. They never gave Rosalind credit for her work or admitted how much they'd learned from it.

James and Francis's paper on the structure of DNA was published in April 1953. Rosalind's papers (she wrote more than one) were published afterward, and they were seen as confirming James and Francis's ideas.

The truth was the other way around.

. . . .

CHAPTER 6

What Rosalind Franklin Means to the World

Rosalind Franklin didn't know that James and Francis based their conclusions on her work. She thought they were working entirely off their own research. She was happy that her research and theirs showed the same thing. That's how scientists know something is true: several people test a question and get the same answer.

Rosalind traveled to Israel to hike around the Dead Sea. She traveled to Europe and the United

States to attend conferences and present her ideas. At Birkbeck College she studied the structure of the tobacco mosaic virus, the first virus ever identified. Rosalind's work helped scientists understand how viruses caused infection and spread.

At Birkbeck, Rosalind wrote seventeen more scientific papers over the next five years. The work she did there was even more impressive than the work she'd done on the structure of DNA.

In 1962, the Nobel Prize in Chemistry was awarded to James Watson, Francis Crick, and Maurice Wilkins for the discovery of the structure of DNA. Rosalind Franklin did not win. For once, this wasn't because she was a woman or because she liked to argue with her fellow researchers. It was because the Nobel Prize can only be given to people who are still living. Rosalind Franklin was dead.

Rosalind had started to feel unwell in 1956. Her stomach swelled as though she was pregnant, but she knew she was not. When doctors operated, they found tumors in her abdomen. Rosalind had ovarian cancer, possibly caused by overexposure to X-rays.

She did not like to talk about it. Very few people even knew she was sick. She kept working, as much as she could, while undergoing treatment. She spent time with her parents, siblings, and nieces and nephews. She died on April 16, 1958, and was buried the next day in a Jewish cemetery in London. She was thirty-seven years old.

For a long time, people forgot about Rosalind Franklin and ignored her many contributions to science. When James Watson wrote his famous book about DNA, *The Double Helix*, he made Rosalind sound absurd. He called her "Rosy," which no one ever did, said she was Maurice Wilkins's assistant, which she was not, and made her sound like a miserable, nasty person instead of a brilliant researcher. Even Maurice, who disliked Rosalind, said the book was made-up.

One of Rosalind's friends, April Sayre, wrote a book defending her. Researchers at King's College read her original notes and realized how groundbreaking her work had been. In 1983, Aaron Klug, who worked with Rosalind at the end of her life, won the Nobel Prize for the work he'd done using X-ray diffraction. If Rosalind were still alive, she might have shared that prize, too. She might have become the only person to win two Nobel Prizes in Chemistry.

Eventually more people heard Rosalind's story. Today she's honored and recognized all over the world. The schools where she studied and worked—St. Paul's Girls' School, Cambridge, King's College, and Birkbeck College—all named buildings after her, and so did many other institutions. There's an asteroid named after her, and also a Cambridge women's racing boat, and the European rover that went to Mars. The Royal Society never admitted her as a member, but they now give a research grant every year in her name. In England's National Portrait Gallery, a painting of Rosalind hangs beside paintings of James Watson, Francis Crick, and Maurice Wilkins. In 2020, to honor what would have been Rosalind's one hundredth birthday, England issued a new

fifty-pence coin. On its reverse side is a copy of Photo 51.

All of those honors are noteworthy, but Rosalind's contributions to science are her real memorial. Once scientists understood the structure of DNA, they started to be able to figure out how it worked. From there they learned how to understand and even treat genetic diseases, such as sickle cell anemia and certain forms of cancer. Now DNA testing can help convict some people of crimes— and prove that others are innocent. Some vaccines, including some of the new ones for COVID-19, were developed in part thanks to DNA research. You can even test your own DNA with at-home kits and find out what countries your ancestors might have come from.

So many people were searching for the structure of DNA that someone was bound to have discovered it eventually. Rosalind Franklin loved to solve problems. She was curious. She worked hard. And she was first.

HOW YOU CAN PERSIST

by Kimberly Brubaker Bradley

Rosalind's discoveries changed the world. Yours might, too! Here are some ways you can persist like Rosalind:

1. Be curious. Ask questions. Look carefully at things. Pay attention to the world around you.

2. Play hard. Rosalind loved sports, games,

and hiking. She loved physical activity. Find ways to move your body that you enjoy.

3. Speak up! Rosalind was never afraid to tell other people what she thought. Stand up for yourself and for what's right. Don't mistake being quiet for being good.

4. Do what you love. Rosalind loved chemistry, math, and physics. You might love butterflies, history, and accounting. Whatever you love, learn as much as you can about it. Enjoy learning. Enjoy making discoveries.

5. Realize how much we still don't know. The discoveries Rosalind made helped change the world for the better. The

world is still changing, and there is still so much to learn. Discoveries you make might cure cancer, destroy pollution, or give people new and beautiful kinds of art. The possibilities are endless.

∽ References ∾

Elkin, Lynne. "Rosalind Franklin and the Double
Helix." *Physics Today* 56, no. 3 (March 2003):
42–48. physicstoday.scitation.org/doi/10.1063
/1.1570771.

Hobbs, Bernie. "The Big and the Small." ABC
Science. Last modified March 30, 2010. abc.net
.au/science/articles/2010/03/30/2859247.htm.

Roach, J. P. C., ed. "The University of
Cambridge: Epilogue (1939–56)," in *A History
of the County of Cambridge and the Isle
of Ely: Volume 3, the City and University of
Cambridge*. Victoria County History: London,
1959. 307–312. british-history.ac.uk/vch/cambs
/vol3/pp307-312.

KIMBERLY BRUBAKER BRADLEY (she/her) is the author of eighteen previous books, including the Newbery Honor winners *Fighting Words* and *The War That Saved My Life*. A chemist by training, she's long admired Rosalind Franklin and is thrilled to be able to tell her story to this audience. The mother of two grown children, she lives with her husband, Bart, on a fifty-two-acre horse farm in northeastern Tennessee with three horses, two dogs, and too many cats.

You can visit Kimberly online at
kimberlybrubakerbradleycom.wordpress.com
and follow her on Twitter and Instagram
@kimbbradley

GILLIAN FLINT has worked as a professional illustrator since earning an animation and illustration degree in 2003. Her work has since been published in the UK, USA and Australia. In her spare time, Gillian enjoys reading, spending time with her family and puttering about in the garden on sunny days. She lives in the northwest of England.

You can visit Gillian Flint online at
gillianflint.com
or follow her on Twitter
@GillianFlint
and on Instagram
@gillianflint_illustration

CHELSEA CLINTON is the author of the #1 *New York Times* bestseller *She Persisted: 13 American Women Who Changed the World*; *She Persisted Around the World: 13 Women Who Changed History*; *She Persisted in Sports: American Olympians Who Changed the Game*; *Don't Let Them Disappear: 12 Endangered Species Across the Globe*; *It's Your World: Get Informed, Get Inspired & Get Going!*; *Start Now!: You Can Make a Difference*; with Hillary Clinton, *Grandma's Gardens* and *Gutsy Women*; and, with Devi Sridhar, *Governing Global Health: Who Runs the World and Why?* She is also the Vice Chair of the Clinton Foundation, where she works on many initiatives, including those that help empower the next generation of leaders. She lives in New York City with her husband, Marc, their children and their dog, Soren.

You can follow Chelsea Clinton on Twitter
@ChelseaClinton
or on Facebook at
facebook.com/chelseaclinton

ALEXANDRA BOIGER has illustrated nearly twenty picture books, including the She Persisted books by Chelsea Clinton; the popular Tallulah series by Marilyn Singer; and the Max and Marla books, which she also wrote. Originally from Munich, Germany, she now lives outside of San Francisco, California, with her husband, Andrea, daughter, Vanessa, and two cats, Luiso and Winter.

Photo credit: *Vanessa Blasich*

You can visit Alexandra Boiger online at
alexandraboiger.com
or follow her on Instagram
@alexandra_boiger

Read about more inspiring women in the

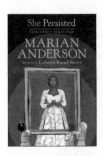

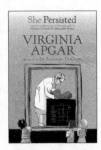

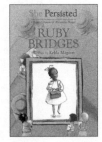

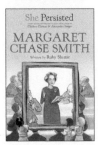

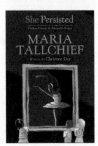

She Persisted series!

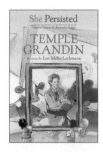

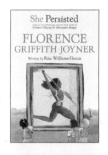

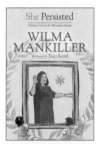

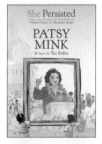

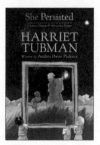